# Welcome to Egypt

## By Patrick Ryan

The Child's World®

Welcome to the WORLD

**Published by The Child's World®**
1980 Lookout Drive
Mankato, MN 56003-1705
800-599-READ
www.childsworld.com

**Content Adviser:** Professor Paul Sprachman, Vice Director,
Center for Middle Eastern Studies, Rutgers, The State University
of New Jersey, New Brunswick, NJ
**Design and Production:** The Creative Spark, San Juan, Capistrano, CA
**Editorial:** Publisher's Diner, Wendy Mead, Greenwich, CT
**Photo Research:** Deborah Goodsite, Califon, NJ

**Cover and title page photo:** Trygve Bolstad/Panos Pictures
**Interior photos:** Alamy: 25 (Jon Arnold Images); AP Photo: 18 top (Hasan Jamali), 19 (Mohamed
El-Dakhakhny), 23 (Ruth Fremson), 24 (Petros Giannakouris); Corbis: 22 (Envision); Getty Images:
8 (Travel Ink/Gallo Images), 3 middle, 9 (Alexander Nesbitt/Aurora); iStockphoto.com: 10 (Karim
Hesham), 3 bottom, 16 (Adrian Beesley), 28 (Ufuk Zivana), 29 (Tim McCaig); Jupiter Images: 20
(Upperhall Ltd/Robert Harding ); Landov: 6 (Tara Todras-Whitehill/ Reuters), 11 (dpa), 13 (UPI), 15
(Xinhua); Panos Pictures: 7 (Mark Henley); Photolibrary Group: 3 top, 14 top, 14 bottom, 27, 30;
SuperStock: 18 bottom (age fotostock).
**Map:** XNR Productions: 5

**Library of Congress Cataloging-in-Publication Data**
Ryan, Patrick, 1948–
  Welcome to Egypt / by Patrick Ryan.
    p. cm. — (Welcome to the world)
  Includes index.
  ISBN 978-1-59296-969-2 (library bound : alk. paper)
 1. Egypt—Juvenile literature.  I. Title. II. Series.

DT49.R974 2008
932—dc22

                                        2007034769

# Contents

# Where Is Egypt?

If you were an astronaut circling Earth, you would see huge land areas surrounded by water. These land areas are called **continents.** One of Earth's continents is Africa. It is made up of many different countries. One large country in the north of the continent of Africa is Egypt.

This picture gives us a flat look at Earth. Egypt is inside the red circle.

Did you **know?**

The country is really called "the Arab Republic of Egypt." People just say "Egypt" for short.

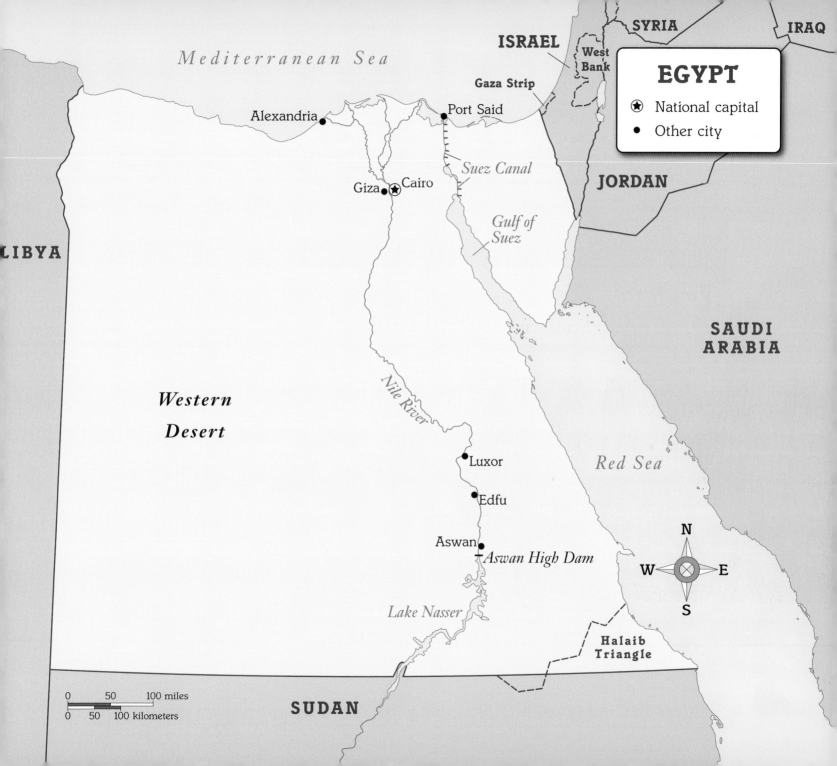

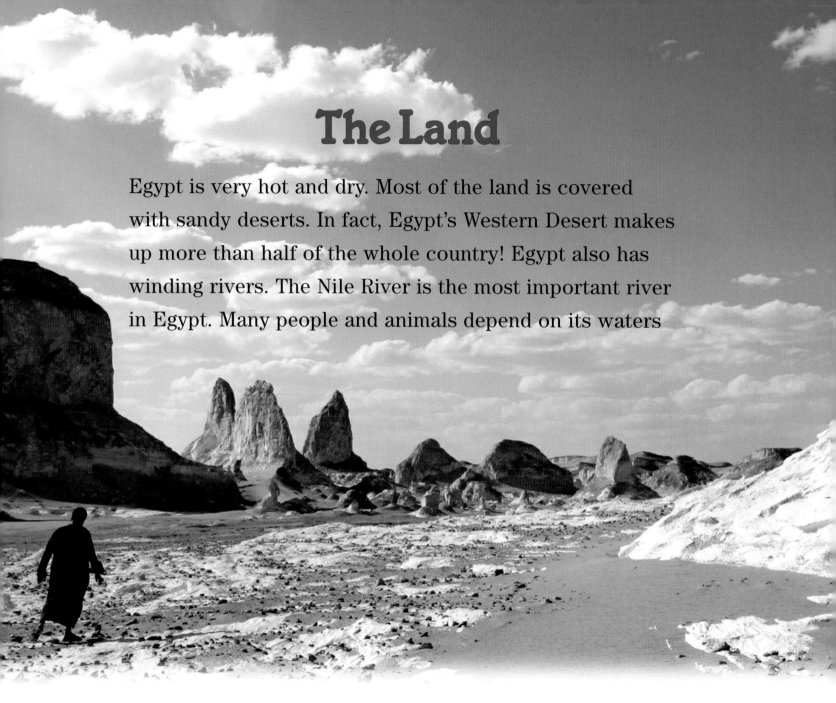

# The Land

Egypt is very hot and dry. Most of the land is covered with sandy deserts. In fact, Egypt's Western Desert makes up more than half of the whole country! Egypt also has winding rivers. The Nile River is the most important river in Egypt. Many people and animals depend on its waters

**Egypt has many deserts, including the White Desert shown here.**

for drinking and cleaning. The Nile is also important because it brings water for Egypt's crops. The Nile is very different from most of the world's rivers. It flows north instead of south.

Men fish on the Nile River.

## Did you know?

An **oasis** is an area in the desert that has water. Water bubbles up from deep underground to make the oasis green with grasses and palm trees. Egypt has several oases. Long ago, wanderers would stop and rest with their camels at these cool "rest stops."

7

# Plants and Animals

An acacia tree

Most of Egypt's plants and trees like the hot, dry weather. Sycamore, tamarisk, and acacia trees all do well in that climate. But near the Nile, different kinds of plants are found. Cypress, eucalyptus, and fruit trees all grow in the rich soil there. Such colorful flowers as lotus and jasmine live along the water's edge.

Many animals make Egypt their home. The most famous of these creatures is the camel. Camels can go for long periods of time without drinking water. Egypt also has many reptiles. Crocodiles and poisonous snakes often live near the Nile River.

8

Camels are often used to travel across Egypt's deserts.

# Long Ago

People have been living in Egypt for a very long time. Thousands of years ago, kings and queens called **pharaohs** ruled the land. The pharaohs lived in fancy palaces and were

**The pyramids of Giza**

very wealthy. When a pharaoh died, he or she was buried in a giant tomb. The tomb was hidden inside a huge stone building called a **pyramid.** Some pyramids were more than 450 feet (137 meters) tall.

## Did you know?

Each year, thousands of people come to see the Great Sphinx in Egypt's desert. Located in Giza, the sphinx is a huge statue that has the head of a person and the body of a lion. It is thought to be a monument to a great pharaoh of long ago. The Great Sphinx is about 4,500 years old.

# Egypt Today

Over the years, the pharaohs lost their power. Other countries began to rule Egypt. After many wars and many years of fighting, the people of Egypt began to rule their own country. Today, Egypt is at peace with its neighbors. It has a president and a prime minister instead of a pharaoh. The president and the prime minister work together with other members of the government to make laws that keep Egypt safe.

Egyptian president Hosni Mubarak casts his vote in the 2005 elections.

# The People

Egypt is a land of old ways and new ways. Some Egyptians live as their grandparents did—in simple homes and raise animals. Others live in big cities with fast cars and busy shops.

The streets of Cairo are often filled with people walking and shopping.

A girl goes for a ride at her family's farm in Edfu.

14

Religion is a very important part of the Egyptian way of life. Most Egyptians are **Muslims.** They pray five times a day. During prayer time, Muslims stop whatever they are doing. They kneel down and pray quietly to themselves. Some Egyptians are Christians called Copts.

A group of Muslims during a time of prayer.

Cairo was established more than 1,000 years ago.

# City Life and Country Life

Less than half of all Egyptians live in cities. The country's biggest city, Cairo, is also its capital. And like other cities of the world, there are problems with pollution. But the government of Egypt is working to make Cairo and other big cities better places to live.

In the countryside, some people are called *fellahin* (feh-luh-HEEN). They often live in brick homes with metal roofs. The Bedouins (BEH-doh-winz) are country people, too. But they are **nomads** (NOH-madz), or wanderers. Instead of houses, Bedouins live in tents. They travel from place to place with their herds of sheep, goats, and camels.

A boy reads a book in Arabic.

# Schools and Language

In many ways, school in Egypt is much like school in the United States. Children learn science, math, social studies, and music just as you do. But on Fridays, Egyptian schools are closed. That is because Fridays are special days of rest for many Egyptian families.

## Did you **know?**

Long ago, Egyptians used a written language called **hieroglyphics (hy-roh-GLI-fiks).** By writing pictures in a certain order, Egyptians could leave messages or tell stories about anything they wanted to.

18

A class of young girls in Cairo

Egypt's official language is Arabic. It is a very old language that has been spoken for thousands of years. Many people also speak English.

19

Many Egyptian farms are near the Nile River.

# Work

Egyptians are good at farming, but the weather is very hot and dry for growing crops. To help their crops grow better, the farmers use pipes to bring water to their fields. This is called **irrigation.** With the help of irrigation, Egyptian farmers raise such crops as sugarcane, cotton, dates, and olives.

Oil is another product of the desert. Oil is very important and is needed for many different things. Most of the oil that comes out of Egypt is sent to special factories that turn it into gas. Then it is sent all over the world to be used by millions of people.

# Food

Egyptian meals are delicious. Many dishes are made with lamb and vegetables. Another popular meal is *ful*, a dish made with beans and tomatoes. Many Egyptians eat this dish every day—even for breakfast. Egyptians also like bread. But Egyptian bread is different. It is flat instead of high and springy. It is sometimes made with eggplant and yogurt.

Some Egyptians start their day with a bowl of *ful*.

A family shares a special holiday meal.

Lots of Egyptian kids like to play soccer.

# Pastimes

Egyptians love to have fun. They often play such sports as tennis, golf, and basketball. They also like to race horses and go sailing on the Nile.

But one of the most popular pastimes is soccer. In Egypt, you can find people playing soccer in the streets, in the schoolyards, and even in the countryside. Soccer is everywhere!

Many people enjoy sailing on the Nile River.

# Holidays

Many of Egypt's holidays are special days in the Muslim religion. Ramadan is a holiday that is about a month long. During Ramadan, Muslims do not eat or drink during the day. They usually have a meal before dawn and another one after dusk. At the end of the month, families join together to share a feast.

Egypt is a land of old and new. Perhaps one day you will visit this sunny land. If you do, remember to smile—its happy people are sure to welcome you!

**Many people attend a festival to celebrate the end of Ramadan.**

# Fast Facts About Egypt

**Area:** More than 386,000 square miles (999,735 square kilometers). That is about the size of Texas and New Mexico put together.

**Population:** About 72 million people

**Capital City:** Cairo

**Other Important Cities:** Alexandria, Giza, Aswan, Luxor

**Money:** The Egyptian pound

**National Language:** Arabic

**National Holiday:** Revolution Day, July 23

**Head of State:** President

**Head of Government:** Prime minister

**National Flag:** Red, white, and black with a golden eagle in the middle. The red stands for Egypt's deserts. The black stands for the rich farmlands near the Nile.

**Famous People:**

**Hatshepsut:** the first female pharaoh

**Sayyed Darweesh:** musician, created the country's current national anthem

**Umm Kulthum:** Egyptian singer

**Naguib Mahfouz:** author

**Hosni Mubarak:** president of Egypt

**Anwar Sadat:** former president of Egypt, Nobel Peace Prize winner

**Ahmed Zewail:** Nobel Prize-winning scientist

**National Song:** *"Belady, Belady, Belady"* ("My Homeland, My Homeland, My Homeland")

My homeland, my homeland, my homeland,
My love and my heart are for thee.
My homeland, my homeland, my homeland,
My love and my heart are for thee

Egypt! O mother of all lands,
My hope and my ambition,
How can one count
The blessings of the Nile for mankind?

My homeland, my homeland, my homeland,
My love and my heart are for thee.
My homeland, my homeland, my homeland,
My love and my heart are for thee

Egypt! Most precious jewel,
Shining on the brow of eternity!
O my homeland, be for ever free,
Safe from every foe!

My homeland, my homeland, my homeland,
My love and my heart are for thee.
My homeland, my homeland, my homeland,
My love and my heart are for thee

Egypt! Noble are thy children,
Loyal, and guardians of thy soil.
In war and peace
We give our lives for thy sake.

My homeland, my homeland, my homeland,
My love and my heart are for thee.

## Egyptian Folklore: The Story of King Tut

Tutankhamen was a young prince in ancient Egypt. He became pharaoh around the age of nine, but only ruled for a short time. He died when he was only 18 years old and was buried in an elaborate tomb more than 3,000 years ago. The story of his brief reign faded over the centuries.

In 1922, a British **archaeologist** named Howard Carter found the long-forgotten tomb of the boy king. Inside he found the mummy of King Tut along with many treasures.

**29**

# How Do You Say...

| ENGLISH | ARABIC | HOW TO SAY IT |
|---|---|---|
| hello | ahlan | AH-lan |
| good-bye | maessalaama | ma-a-sah-LEH-muh |
| please | min fadlak | min FAD-lak |
| thank you | shukran | SHU-kran |
| one | wehid | WEH-hid |
| two | itneyn | it-NEYN |
| three | talehta | ta-LEH-ta |
| Egypt | masr | ma-SIR |

# Glossary

**archaeologist (ar-kee-OL-uh-jist)** A person who studies the sites and materials from the past. Many archaeologists have examined the pyramids and items found there to learn about the ancient Egyptians.

**continents (KON-tih-nents)** The largest land areas on Earth are called continents. Egypt is on the continent of Africa.

**hieroglyphics (hy-roh-GLI-fiks)** Long ago, Egyptians used a kind of writing called hieroglyphics. It used shapes and pictures instead of words.

**irrigation (eer-ih-GAY-shun)** Irrigation uses pipes and pumps to bring water to fields. Many Egyptian farmers must use irrigation or their crops will die.

**Muslims (MUHS-lihms)** Followers of the Islamic religion are called Muslims. Most Egyptians are Muslims.

**nomads (NOH-madz)** Nomads are people who travel from place to place instead of settling down. Nomads in Egypt travel with their herds of goats and sheep.

**oasis (oh-AY-sis)** An oasis is an area in the desert that has water. An oasis is often green with grass and trees.

**pharaohs (FAIR-ohz)** Long ago, the rulers of Egypt were called pharaohs. Pharaohs lived in fancy palaces and were very wealthy.

**pyramid (PEER-uh-mid)** A pyramid is one of the huge triangle shaped buildings that were built long ago. The pyramids in Egypt were used as tombs for the pharaohs.

31

# Further Information

## Read It

Gibbons, Gail. *Mummies, Pyramids, and Pharaohs: A Book About Ancient Egypt.* New York: Little, Brown, 2004.

Hart, George. *Ancient Egypt.* New York: DK Publishing, 2004.

Hobbs, Joseph J. and Aswin Subanthore. *Egypt.* New York: Chelsea House, 2007.

## Look It Up

Visit our Web page for lots of links about Egypt:
**http://www.childsworld.com/links**

*Note to Parents, Teachers, and Librarians:* We routinely verify our Web links to make sure they are safe, active sites—so encourage your readers to check them out!

# Index